FLAWED TO MASTERPIECE SERIES BOOK 2

WHY DID YOU MARRY ME?

A must-read for all women!

Sherilyn L Fletcher

Why did you marry me?

ISBN 9798642458273

Dedication

I dedicate first to the Holy Spirit, my commander, and chief. To my children Deltera, Keishan, DeArana, Keirano, Dekeira, William. My adopted babies Charles and Honesty, I love you all!

Table of Contents

PREFACE

Preface

This book was inspired by my struggles, with no one to share my efforts. My gifts and talents were more critical than my lifestyle. There were many days I wanted to commit suicide. I didn't think I was going to make it this far, thank God I'm here. Many women are desperate to get married, not paying attention to the warning signs or waiting on God

I wanted to share my story, so others would know they are not alone.

Your Proverbs 31 man will find you!

Chapter 1

Am I not good enough for marriage?

I grew up in a very verbally, abusive home. I find myself even now having to ask God to help me choose my words wisely, especially when I'm upset. I hated my life. I would sometimes speculate about death. We didn't know how to show love or comfort to each other in that home. Instead, we hurled nasty, hurtful words at one another. Laughter and mockery were our way of supporting someone that was hurting. Love, validation, and words of encouragement were foreign to my family. It took years for me to learn how to receive a compliment from someone. I am the eighth child of the nine children born to the same mother and father.

I have seven brothers and one sister, both my parents are now deceased. My family was big, yet most of my life, I felt I was always the oddball. My family was impoverished;

we had to depend on our mother each day for meals. Whatever she was able to purchase, she cooked, and we could decide to eat it or go to bed hungry. I couldn't wait to leave home and start my dream life with my future husband. I felt if I were out of the house, away from my family, my life would be better. Sometimes I wondered if I was an alien, belonging to another world; because of the way I was treated. My life consisted of a church, school, and home; there were no social outings.

My knowledge of sex, pregnancy, and diseases was next to nothing; I didn't have an excellent example of how a marital home operates successfully; I only knew abuse. My father abused my mother physically and verbally, and some of my brothers followed his example in their marriages.

I was in the twelfth grade when I met a boy from my church name Delphin. His father was a minister at our local assembly, a man of integrity.

I spoke to my mother about him wanting to date me, and she gave consent. My father was never around and never seemed to care about anyone or anything. Within the months of dating, I became pregnant in the month of my graduation from high school. I was so afraid to tell my parents, not knowing what the response was going to be. I grew up in an era where children were supposed to be seen and not heard. On several occasions, I tried to have that conversation with my mom about the birds and the bees. I was shut down each time and told me I was too fresh (grown). When the day I decided to tell her came about my condition, I was terrified. She was outside hanging up clothes on the line in the backyard. I started out asking her how she was doing, you know, looking for an opening. Then I blurted it out, "Mommy, I'm pregnant, "there I thought to myself I said it. I waited for a response. She became hysterical, "oh my God, your father is going to kill you and me." I begin to panic; what I'm I going to do? I should run away. I cannot stay here; he's going to kill me. Thoughts were flying through my mind, and I could not eat or sleep that night. My mom never told me if she said my father, he never said anything to me about it.

Delphin was supportive during my pregnancy, and he took good care of me, providing my needs. I was extremely sick during this pregnancy, couldn't eat or drink anything except milk.

After some time, my mother scheduled a meeting with his parents to discuss his intentions for me. Wow, my fairytale dream is about to happen. I am finally leaving this house. Delphin was not present during the meeting with his parents, my mother, and me. His mother spoke up for him, and boldly declared he said: "he is not ready to get married." She later stated that she was not forcing him and further insulted me by stating she needed to wait for the baby to be born to ensure it was his. I thought I was dreaming, pinch me, slap me, someone; please tell me to wake up. I felt like I was dreaming. I sunk into a deep depression, anger, and frustration, taking turns simultaneously. My dreams of marrying my baby's father tainted by the hurtful words that came from Delphin's mother. I had so many unanswered questions, continually running through my mind.

I came home from the antenatal clinic one day, exhausted from walking in the hot sun. I met two of my brothers sitting in the living room, engaged in a conversation. As I walked through the door, an outburst of laughter came from them " you are such a fool you will suffer," says one " you will come to me begging for money to buy food for that baby, " laughter continues. I didn't respond; I made up in my mind at the moment that I would never succumb to their wishes for my life

Delphin and I remained together, despite his decision. He told me he would marry me later after the baby was born. On March 3rd, I gave birth to a beautiful baby girl; it was a happy day for me. She was the smallest, most beautiful creature I have ever seen. I could not keep my eyes off her. I wanted the world to see my beautiful baby.

My mother was a powerful woman of God; I would hear her praying all the time for her children. She never verbally abused her children. She neglected us because she had to provide for us. She never showed the love that I needed as a little girl; she did what she knew. I wanted my baby to know and experience my love for her. I decided I wanted to get a job to support myself and the baby. The words of my brothers rang in my head always.

Delphin's entire attitude towards me started to change, slowly, after I got a job. The first was when he decided not to take part in the baby's dedication. He came to church that day and refused to be a part of the ceremony or pictures. God, how much more can I take? Why am I here? When will my story change? Questions I'm sure most of you reading have asked on many occasions. We are created for a purpose. When the purpose is not fulfilled or on the path to achieving that, it can be very taxing on our emotions. Humankind was born with specific instructions, to operate in the earth realm; anything outside of that gives us a sense of emptiness.

"Hey, Delphin, I noticed you no longer giving me money to help take care of the baby."

His response cut me to the core. He told me, " since you're working, take care of the child yourself." Delphin started to talk down to me, calling me ugly and stating how repulsive it was to even get into a relationship with me. Yet I remained in this now physical and verbally abusive relationship. On one occasion, he beat me up because I bought a cute outfit and was receiving compliments everywhere we went. I started to believe failure was my destiny. My drive to take care of my daughter and I catapulted me to another level of perseverance. She was all

I had in the whole wide world. I knew in my mind that Delphin was not going to marry me, and it was time to move on with my life. There is still hope, after all, I was still young. When I told Delphin about my intentions to end the relationship, he was furious and began to hurl insults at me. "you could never make it without me, why don't you wait for me, I am going to marry you!" I must pause right here to encourage you reading this book, always remember who God says you are;

Psalms 139:14

14 I will praise thee; for I am fearfully and wonderfully made: marvelous are thy works; and that my soul knoweth right well.

You are important and, just because you may or may not have it together right now doesn't change whom God has made you become. Don't ever give a man all the boons of what it is to be for a married couple and expect him to make it legitimate in the eyes of the Lord. There is a saying, "why buy the cow when one can get the milk for free." Take a moment, look into the mirror, say these words, "I am beautiful inside and out because God made me. I will succeed because my father is the Lord, and he is the creator of the universe. This situation will pass, watch and see {insert name} you will survive this."

Prayer Point for God's divine choice of a life partner

It is important to pray before one embarks on having a relationship with anyone. These prayer points will guide you to pray the word. We don't know what to pray, the Holy Spirit makes intercession for you and me.

Every power of my father's house and mother's house that is making me look older, uglier, unattractive before my husband/partner, catch fire and die, in the name of Jesus.

I shall not spend the whole of this year searching for the right husband in Jesus name

My Father, among of these men asking for my hands in marriage, show me the right husband, in Jesus name

My Father, Help me not to use my sentiment to choose the wrong husband, in Jesus' name O God, look at my direction today because no man is asking for my hands in marriage, in Jesus' name.

O Lord, If I have offended you to deserve this lateness in marriage, Father have mercy upon me in Jesus name

Father, I have attended lots of people's marriage; by Your divine arrangement, let my right husband attract them to celebrate with me in Jesus' name.

My Father, reveal to me the thing or personality that want me to be unfortunate in marital breakthrough, in Jesus name

My Father, despite my beauty, money, accommodation, I can't still find the right husband who will love me wholeheartedly, Dear Lord, locate him for me, in Jesus name

My Father, I am hungry and thirsty for true marriage. Please do something concerning my marriage before.......(choose a date), so that I can be a proud mother, in Jesus name
O Lord, talk to me to know if you still want me to marry or not. My Father, who is my right husband? Speak to me in a clear matter.

My Father, by fire by force, you must take me to the place where my right husband is located in this country, in Jesus name

O Lord, I am simply tired of rising and fall relationships in the hands of fake men.

Reveal to me Your choice for my life, in Jesus' name My Father, You said in your word, He that findeth a wife, findeth a good thing and obtaineth favor from the Lord.

Do you want me to search for men? My Father, as the earth remaineth, anyone that is secretly bringing me and my right partner under the bondage of the devil, Holy Ghost fire destroy them in Jesus name

O Lord, If it is a spirit husband that is preventing me from getting married, let it be destroyed in Jesus' name.

Right before the eyes of my enemy, I shall marry, in the name of Jesus.

Household powers stopping me from meeting my life partner, die in Jesus name.
Every confusing demon, narrating my life to my fiance, be frustrated in Jesus name
I shall not be deceived by men in the name of Jesus.

Evil powers working day and night to see that I remain unmarried, scatter by fire, in Jesus name
My Father, let the spirit of anger in my life, be destroyed in Jesus name

I shall not marry the enemy as a husband, in Jesus name

Every time-consuming man assigned to delay my marriage, be wasted in Jesus name
Every dream of spiritual marriage, I cancel it in the name of Jesus.

Whether the devil or not, I shall be located this year in Jesus name

My Father, help me to promote my courtship or relationship into a Godly marriage, in Jesus name

Old age thoughts holding me in one spot, release me by fire, in Jesus name

What happened to my parents during their marital challenge will not affect me, in Jesus name

Any idols of my father's that say my family must worship them before they can release the key of my marriage, you are a liar, release them and catch fire, in the name of Jesus.

Evil powers in my family holding the key of my marital joy and victory, what are you waiting for? release it and die, in the name of Jesus.

Holy Ghost, pull me out from the valley of confusion and frustration, in the name of Jesus.

Premarital Counseling Questionnaire

Below are some questions that can be used in your time or at a Women's Fellowship. We must do a deep soul searching before we say I do

1. Name Two Characteristics Which You Admire In Your Mate or mate to be.

_____

2. Name two characteristic or weakness, which you least appreciate about your mate

_____

3. Are you well acquainted with your mate's immediate family? Describe your relationship to them.

_____

_____

_____

4. Give Five Reasons for Wanting To Marry.

a.

b.

c.

d.

e.

5. How long have you known each other?

_____

6. How long have you been engaged?

_____

7. Does your family approve completely of your mate?

_____

8. What would you consider grounds for divorce?

_____

9. For what reasons do you think divorce rate continues to increase?

Chapter 2

Why did you marry me?

In June 1988, Wendy's old-fashioned hamburgers came to the beautiful shores of the Bahamas. I was a part of the original crew hired. My daughter was getting older; I needed more income. I had worked as a maid but was unsuccessful as the woman of the house kept accusing me of not completing the tasks; she had asked me to do. It became unbearable and uncomfortable. One day I called her after we had had a few days of heavy rain. She told me she would call if she needed me. I never received that call. When I first applied for a position at Wendy's, I waited daily anxiously, hoping to receive a call from the agency. I had no help as I said before my family was impoverished; my mother was doing her best to keep a roof over our heads and food on the table. I finally received the call after I had the interview for Wendy's that I was going to be a part of the crew. Wow! Something is finally working for me! After I got paid every week, I was left with a few dollars, having to purchase food and pay the babysitter. I cried for many weeks because of this, but I was determined to take care of my baby. My life was dull, just work and home, I had no social experience.

My brother, who is a few years older than I am, stopped attending church. He was now a part of a world that was foreign to me. One night he asked me to go with him to the nightclub, he explained to me the fun he was having and that I would enjoy it as well. Enthused by his stories, I wanted to experience what he was sharing with me. I still had to persuade my mom to let me go out even though I was off age and had a child. My brother convinced her for about an hour that we were going to a church birthday party. She finally gave in and agreed to keep my baby. That was the worst decision she made that night. My life changed drastically after that night; I no longer wanted to stay home. The loud music, the dancing, the drinking (well the alcohol was nasty at first) intrigued me. What is this world? Did I die and go to heaven? I danced the entire night, that was one of the happiest moment of my life. Every day after I got off from work, I was looking for a nightclub to attend seven days a week. I no longer had time for my daughter; I had found a new life, a new way to bury my sorrow. The more I drank alcohol, the better it tasted; this was my anesthesia against the pain life had dealt me. My mother had no more control over my coming in and going out. The nightlife was my new best friend.

Then I met him, he was dark and handsome, seemed kind and sincere. Remember, I did not know what to expect from a man or what to give or not give. 'Would you like to dance?' He asked, Sure! I responded. He escorted me to the floor, and we danced the entire night, fast songs, slow songs, happy and sad songs. We drank together, laughed together, it was a warm moment. After speaking with him briefly, I realized we shared similar pain from past

24

relationships. Let me explain something to you, getting into another relationship without first being healed from past hurts will only cause your sorrow to deepen. Many times, one would get into another relationship as a rebound. You see, Phillip, and I already had so much baggage we were still carrying. His childhood consists of verbal and sexual abuses, and like me, he was already using a sedative to numb the pain. Over the months, we started to spend more time together, engaging in sexual acts to attempt to satisfy one another. Sex is another sedative used by many to numb the pain one faces. Phillip was a product of a one-parent home; he barely knew his father, his mother mistreated him. His mother's brother was molesting Philip, and most of his siblings, she knew about it and did nothing. She would still leave him and his siblings' home with her brother to babysit while she was at work.

There are many relationships where one of the partners uses sex to manipulate the other person's love for them.

Sex will never be equal to love. Love is the ability to have a deep feeling of fondness for a person is; love accepts the strengths and the shortcomings of an individual. Your body is valuable, a treasure that all the money in the world cannot purchase. A girl needs the validation from her father, brother, or uncle; without this, that girl will never know her worth and would become callous, with low self-esteem or promiscuousness. How can a man find her as a wife, when she has no idea what it means to be a wife. Young girls need opportunities to have to mentor on how and what to do to become successful as a wife and mother. Most importantly, how to become a child of God.

Philip was already talking about marriage after three months into our relationship. I was so excited, I'm getting married! I knew my dreams would come through one day; things are finally looking up. I got a new job, found a new world and now a new man. I told my mom about his intentions; she was happy for me (I believe she wanted me gone as much as I wanted to go :) That day she sat both of us down and gave us godly advice, as any good mother would do. My friend, who graduated with me from school, he became one of my drinking partners. He was not pleased with my decision to marry someone I barely knew. I ignored all negative voices at this point; I was getting married. God always shows us signs before we get into relationships with someone, but because of desperation, blind to the truth, and lack of value for ourselves, we ignore those signs.

Amos 3:7

Indeed, the Lord GOD does nothing without revealing His counsel to his servants, the prophets.

2 Corinthians 2:11

Lest Satan should get an advantage of us: for we are not ignorant of his devices.

Pay close attention to the signs; don't ignore them. Ladies, we somehow feel we can cause a man to change after he is married or if I get pregnant for him. God gives us guidelines in his word on how we should conduct ourselves as women.

Proverbs 31:10-31

An excellent wife who can be found? She is far more precious than jewels. The heart of her husband trusts in her, and he will have no lack of gain. She does him good and not harm all the days of her life. She seeks wool and flax and works with willing hands. She is like the ships of the merchant; she brings her food from afar.

By this time, I had met Philip's mother, who was not fond of me being in her son's life. We spoke to her and his siblings about the plans to get married. We were inviting them to be a part of this occasion. Before we could even continue with the conversation, she shouted, "I'm not going," because, "I don't agree with this marriage." What a blow, but I shook it off and continued to think about my big day. This refusal to attend or support her son's wedding was another sign; I ignored, I just wanted to be married free from my family.

I remember the day Philip proposed, I was off that day at home relaxing. He bought me a gift; it was a handbag. As I was looking through the bag, I found it, yes, the ring it was official now. It was happening. I was getting married. Philip was in a relationship with a girl for about six years. She had lied to him about being the father of her child. Three years after the child was born, his biological father came and claimed his son while Philip was sitting in the living room of his girlfriend's house. He was crushed, devastated by her betrayal.

A few weeks before the wedding, she told him she was pregnant for him and was expecting real soon. He was skeptical at first but soon believed her; I realized after we separated, he had still loved her. At that time I was not going to let anything stop me from marrying this man. I ignored the signs. The day before the wedding that she told him had delivered a baby girl. I should have run like Joseph, upon hearing this. I was young, ignorant, and had to figure out things for myself. I didn't receive any good advice, and I choose to ignore them all. I was adamant about marrying Philip. I am writing this book to let you know you have help. Life is a cycle, and I know pride will make us feel or think we will not incur the same results as I did.

"I'm smarter than that; My man already shows me he truly loves me; I've been in a relationship with him for years; People are just jealous, or his family loves me dearly."

These are some of the things we tell ourselves, to convince ourselves that we have made the right decision, the plain and simple truth is we are in denial when one refuses to accept the fact. I've learned over the years that God was always with me, showing me ways of escape, but I choose ignorantly to go the other way.

1 Corinthians 10:13

No temptation has overtaken you except as is common to man; but God is faithful, who will not allow you to be tempted beyond what you are able, but with the temptation will also make the way of escape, that you may be able to bear it.

I was rushing around trying to do my final errands for my wedding day. I remember at the last minute I had to go to the dressmaker to pick up my dress. I wanted my dress custom made for my big day. I was shocked as I looked at the horrible Dressmaker did on my dress. It was as if she allowed her ten-year daughter old to sew it for me. It was ruined and looked nothing like the picture I had given to her. I began to cry, my schoolmate, who was my maid of honor encouraged me just to take the dress and leave. It was too late to fix it or use another avenue. This misfortune was another sign looking, now back at it. Don't get me wrong this happens to couples who are divinely connected. Signs like these show that either God is trying to tell you something or Satan trying to keep you from your divine destiny. It is so essential for you to pray to ensure the man is God's right choice for you. I was desperate to fulfill my dream of being married, so I ignored all the signs.

The next day was my wedding day, and my life is about to change. The church was filled with family and friends that came to support. My father proudly walked me down the aisle to begin my new life with my husband. I was so happy I finally was seeing brighter days, regardless of all the obstacles that were in my way. I looked in the seat reserved for our immediate families, hoping that his mom and siblings would change their minds. The seats were empty; they had not shown up. Oh well, their loss, I was determined to enjoy my day. The ceremony was excellent; the reception was well put together. I was now happily married.

We moved in with my mother for a few weeks until our apartment was ready. One of the managers I worked with had an aunt who had a vacant apartment, not far from my parent's home. Before we moved in, we financed new furniture for the entire house; I was super excited. What could go wrong?

Shortly into our marriage, my husband got into an altercation with his baby mother. She no longer wanted him in her daughter's life; he decided it was time for me to get pregnant. That was music to my ears; he wanted me to carry his child. By November, I was pregnant with our first child, and things were looking up, seemingly. My husband was still clubbing and drinking alcoholic beverages. He was not satisfied with being at home with me. He was burying his sorrows and pains using alcohol. He would come home just about every day, initiating an argument. It was one thing after the next, and there was little peace. Regardless, he made sure he paid all the bills in the house.

He was an excellent provider and protector, but then something happened. He had reconciled with his baby mother and was now back in his daughter's life. My husband came home one day from work, asking if his daughter can come over to spend some time with us. I agreed with this idea; then one day turned into a week. He approached me one evening when I was in the kitchen cooking to ask if his daughter can live with us. I was torn because I already had an eighteen months baby and pregnant with one. This was too much for me to handle. Furthermore, he hardly helped with taking care of the kids. I worked a tedious nine hours every day, standing on my feet most of the time. When I got home, I am tired. My response was 'no way"; she can visit but not live. I cannot take care of her with all the challenges I am faced with right now. He became furious, rushed into our bedroom, and began packing my daughter and my clothes. He flung them outside onto the grass lawn, screaming at the top of his voice, "if my daughter cannot live here, then yawl have to leave.' I did just that, picked up all my clothing, and with tears rolling down, my face drove two corners away to my parent's house. I was so embarrassed; I'm sure my neighbors, especially my manager's friend, saw this.

Days later, Phillip came to my parent's house, apologizing for what he had done. He asked me to go back home, which I did. This time the abuse was now physical; he would hit me for the least things. One time we were in an argument, so I took off my ring. When he got home, he saw it and flew off the handle. I was at my friend's house at the time, just chilling with them. He pulled up, jumped out of the van, and proceeded towards me; I sensed the anger in his eyes, so I ran. He caught me and began to beat me, pushing me, a pregnant lady, on the floor. My friend was trying to stop him in vain; he dragged me into the van and sped off. When we got home, he went ballistic over the fact I took off the ring. I now realized he was still hurting from his past relationship from rejection and betrayal. He told me the next time you take off that ring, I will kill you. I was so depressed, and I was vulnerable.

The vulnerability can cause a person to make real hasty decisions or be taken advantage of if you encounter the wrong people. It is especially important to allow oneself to go through a process of healing, evaluate the pros and cons. Look at what you could have done better and how you can improve. Yes, it is not all about what your partner did to you; you will never heal or move forward positively if you stay in a place of regret, anger, or revenge. Forgiveness helps you more than it does the other person. True forgiveness is when we no longer allow what has happened to us to affect the way we treat the trespasser. The Holy Spirit is our helper, and only he can help us truly forgive those deep-rooted hurts and pains.

My husband spent very little time home, and when he did go out, he would come back, he was always drunk. God, what did I do to make you hate me this much? Why is my life filled with so much pain?

It is only so much a person can take; I decided I was going to my parent's house for a break. As I was leaving in my car, he ran outside, opened the door, and began threatening me to stop, or he would kill me. I stopped the car and reversed in our driveway to keep the peace. I was tired of the embarrassment this was too much for me. I cried the entire night because of all I was facing in this marriage.

I have seven brothers; none came to my rescue; no one tried to counsel or hope us in any way. One day while I was at my parent's house, he came storming inside, I was with one of my brothers in the backroom. He was accusing me of doing something, I am not even sure what it was, and without warnings, he grabbed my brother's flute and began beating me with it until it blended. My brother stood there laughing at me; I don't know what was more painful, the hit or the laughter.

I started drinking again, to hide, or run away in my mind from all that was taking place. It was either around the middle of December when my husband walked out of my life. I asked him why you married me; the response I got almost gave me a heart attack. "I only married you to get back to my girlfriend for what she did to me. I don't love you. I better not see you dating anyone else, or I will hurt you

Then he was gone, just as quickly as he came. I went through all of this in only three months.

After moving back with my parents, I tried never to stay home; I was out drinking and partying every night. I was pregnant with my second child; she didn't deserve all the toxins I was putting in her systems. Depression and suicidal thoughts seem to have escalated in my life. I probably would have attempted suicide if I was not pregnant.

My phone rang early one morning, hello? Hey this me Philip, I just called to let you know what an old whore you are, and I don't believe the baby is mine. You're stupid and have no life; you're riding around with your friends; maybe one of them is the father. I never responded, but for some strange reason, I would pick up the phone every time he called and just listen to him hurl insults at me. I was still hopeful we could work our problems out. I was disappointed each time I answered the call. He did this routine until my daughter was born on August 14th. This baby girl had so much exposure to alcohol; I was in the nightclub dancing all through my pregnancy, smoking, and drinking. Remember, we are a spirit; we live in a body, and we possess a soul. Spiritually all that was I doing; it was becoming a part of her DNA. I was young and ignorant, with little guidance. People often ask me why do you care about people so much, my response is because if I can help someone make better choices than I did, I am willing to try my very best. I know what it feels like to be alone and rejected; many will not and have not survived all that I

39

have gone through. Our testimony helps others more than we know; it is essential to be transparent.

After I gave birth to my daughter, my husband called asking to see the child. I don't know how he found out, but I agreed. He came over, asked me to hold her, looking at her all over after a few minutes he said she did not look like me and left. Nothing he did surprise me anymore; he was still in a relationship with his ex-girlfriend. I was left to raise my two girls alone.

Prayer Points for a new direction

1. *All my blessings imprisoned by the grave, come forth, in the name of Jesus.*

2. *I release my blessings from the hands of my dead relatives, in the name of Jesus.*

3. *I withdraw my blessings from the hands of all dead enemies, in the name of Jesus.*

4. *I disgrace every witchcraft burial, in the name of Jesus.*

5. *Just as the grave could not detain Jesus, no power will detain my miracles, in the name of Jesus.*

6. *That which hinders me from greatness, give way now, in Jesus' name.*

7. *Whatsoever has been done against me, using the ground, be neutralized, in the name of Jesus.*

8. *Every unfriendly friend, be exposed, in the name of Jesus.*

9. *Anything representing my image in the spirit world, I withdraw you, in the name of Jesus.*

10. *All the camps of my enemies receive confusion, in the name of Jesus.*

11. *O Lord, empower my life with Your authority over every demonic force, in Jesus' name.*

12. O Lord, let all the impossible begin to become possible for me in every department of my life, in Jesus' name.

13. O Lord, take me from where I am to where You want me to be.

14. O Lord, make a way for me where there is no way.

15. O Lord, grant me the power to be fulfilled, successful and prosperous in life, in the name of Jesus

16. I claim supernatural wisdom to answer all questions in a way that will advance my cause, in the name of Jesus.

17. I confess my sins of exhibiting occasional doubts.

18. I bind every spirit manipulating my beneficiaries against me, in the name of Jesus.

19. I remove my name from the book of those who see better without tasting it, in the name of Jesus.

20. You the cloud, blocking the sunlight of my glory and breakthrough, disperse, in the name of Jesus.

21. O Lord, let wonderful changes begin to be my lot from this week.

22. I reject every spirit of the tail in all areas of my life, in the name of Jesus.

23. Oh Lord, bring me into favor with all those who will decide on my advancement.

24. Oh Lord, cause a divine substitution to happen to move me ahead.

25. I reject the spirit of the tail, and I claim the spirit of the head, in the name of Jesus.

26. All evil records, planted by the devil in anyone's mind against my advancement, shatter to pieces, in the name of Jesus.

27. Oh Lord, transfer, remove or change all human agents that are bent on stopping my advancement.

28. Oh Lord, smoothen my path to the top by Your hand of fire.

29. I receive the anointing to excel above my contemporaries, in the name of Jesus.

30. O Lord, catapult me into greatness as You did for Daniel in the land of Babylon.

Premarital Counseling Questionnaire

Below are some questions that can be used in your time or at a Women's Fellowship. We must do a deep soul searching before we say I do.

10. Is there anything that makes you jealous of your mate?

_____

11. What are your goals or aims in life? Have you discussed these with your mate?

_____

12. How much education have you had?

_____

13. What is your opinion of household duties?

_____

14. Give a brief physical history of your family.

_____

_____

15. What are two activities (recreation, social, etc.) which you have in common?

_____

16. Do you dislike any of your mate's family or friends?

_____

Chapter 3

Mama's Boy

My life had taken a downward spiral. I continue to drink every day and club every night. Alcohol had become the new norm for me, and I couldn't live without it. Despite all my relationship failures, one thing was sure I was a hard worker. My hard work paid off; I got promoted in Wendy's after six months of being there. I was relaxed about the news that I should have celebrated. I worked hard to take care of my children. Philip was now out of my life for good. I was sunk so deep in depression; I was not sure I would ever come out.

My niece was dating a guy who introduced me to his first cousin Donald. She felt sorry for me and wanted me to go out with her so I could start dating again. I was told we were stopping by his cousin's house to hang out for a bit. His cousin was a very tall guy, not good looking but very clean and neat. We became friends almost instantaneously;

eventually, he became my new drinking buddy. I began to hang out at his place a lot, drinking with them whenever I got a chance. Donald and I became close, over months of us hanging out. His home was the spot where we all hung out on the weekends. He approached me about taking our relationship to another level; he wanted more than friendship. I was so gullible it was pathetic; anyone could take advantage of me because I was and still so trusting. I try to believe the best in people, even though I may see some signs of something different.

There was a young lady who visited him occasionally; I did not care because I was there to hang out and drink. When he confronted me about wanting us to have a relationship, I asked about the young lady. He told me she was just a friend. She would bring new clothing items for him and sometimes food for us all but never hung out with us, so I believed him. Word on the street was she was pregnant, I asked him about it, and he finally said 'he had slept with her twice, but she was already pregnant when it happened. I was already in a relationship with him when I found this out. Did I run, no, of course, didn't even see the warning signs, I was clueless. All I wanted was to love and be loved; why was this so hard to do ugggh. I'll tell you why that image we have in our heads as little girls are not real; even if you have a good marriage, you have to put work on it. When you come from a deep place of rejection and no validation in your life, it leaves you open to wolves and bears. Anyone comes along and shows you a little attention you accept because we want to belong.

Genesis 2:18

And the LORD God said, "It is not good that man should be alone; I will make him a helper comparable to him."

Women, we are created as a helpmate for our husbands. I believe God has the right person for everyone if we follow his path.

Men are hunters, and they love going after a woman that seems adamant about giving them a chance. Women like who I was, were used as sex toys never taken seriously; we always seemed desperate. Desperation turns a man away from a woman; he will only sleep with you because of his ego, trust me; that is all it meant just sex. We are so emotional; we feel we have made a connection through a sexual encounter, and we are in love. He will surely love me now if I give him my pride. Men become suspicious when a woman freely gives herself away without or little resistance. Their minds are so different from ours even though they are encouraging you to sleep with them, they will continue to reap from the well, giving you false hope. Women that are prostitutes are using drugs or some other form of sedative to block out the emotional part of their sexual encounters. Women are receivers or incubators; we can quickly become soul tied with someone that is not our spouse. Back in the day, women tried to trap a man into marrying her by intentionally getting pregnant. As we can see the statistics, that does not work and will never work. We must take account of the word of God

Proverbs 18:22

He who finds a wife finds a good thing and receives favor from the Lord.

Anyway, back to the tea, I hope I made you smile right there, you are going to make it. Do not give up hope, put your trust in God; he will see you through. If you don't have a relationship with Jesus, let me tell you, girl, you're missing out. Okay, for real, let us get back to Donald, and I adventure.

Our friendship was extraordinarily strong because Donald and I were friends before we were lovers. He was a lot of fun to be around and was easy to talk to; I could tell him anything.

He was very caring and loving, as they always are in the beginning right, anyways he was good for me.

The young lady stopped coming around, so I thought nothing about it. Our relationship was growing more reliable, even though my friends would laugh at me, stating how ugly he was. It did not matter to me; I found love; no one was going to separate us.

I had gotten another promotion at Wendy's to become a store manager; things were changing. I found out around the same time I was pregnant for Donald; I can't have this baby, I thought to myself. I spoke to Donald about aborting the baby because I wanted the position, and I was not ready to have another child. We both agreed to abort the child. I remember the day at the clinic; I was terrified this was my first time in an abortion clinic. I woke up crying after the procedure; a nurse ran over to me, asking me if I was okay. I assured her I was okay, but I wasn't, how could you murder your child in cold blood? I was thinking to myself.

We drove home in silence. Donald was concerned about me, so I spent the night in his place.

I moved on rather suddenly feeling no remorse for what I had done, my heart was becoming cold and hardened. A year later, we moved in together, but he still slept at his place. I knew he was cheating on me, but he never got caught. His family would tell me that he was cheating. I stayed with him because there was no proof. I had by now met his mother and sisters, aunts and uncles, we were taking this to the next level for sure.

I began to realize that his sister was frequently upset with their mother because her son could do no wrong. Whatever he told her was gospel, even if the evidence proved different. He was her only son; she had three girls, who were all doing very well.

A year after the abortion, I became pregnant again; this time, I was keeping the baby.

My relationship with Donald was not the best, but we kept working at it.

Then he proposed to me, but for some odd reason, I was not happy. I just knew deep; I was not going to marry him. I went along with it anyway, his mom and everyone else was happy. Communication with my family was next to nothing. They were on a need to know basis, which was never. My sweet mother though I told her all my moves, I still always wanted her blessings. I never hated her for all she did to me; I knew that was God keeping me. She was incredibly happy for me and congratulated me; she was still upset that I moved out and took my two girls. My mom felt I was irresponsible and not mature enough to do so. She was wrong. I made sure my children had what they needed, spend time with them, love them, and put them in good private schools. Every relationship I went in the first thing I told the man was "I want you to take a moment to look me in my eyes, if you ever touched any of my daughters in the wrong way, I will kill you."I never had a problem with any of my kids getting molested, thank God. He needed me out of prison because he knew one day, I would change my life around and help others.

I had done so much to try to help Donald, renovate the building his father had left for him and his siblings. He was running a small business in which I funded.

One thing life had not done was to stop me from being ambitious. I decided I was going to build a house for my kids and me on the property my mom had gotten from the government when our home was destroyed by fire when I was a little girl.

You may not believe in angels, but they exist and can manifest in human form. I cannot tell you why I had to take a taxi home from work because I always had a car. I was in Mr. Brown's taxi, one night, I don't remember the details of the conversation. I mentioned to him I wanted to build an apartment. Mr. Brown explained to me what I needed to accomplish my goals without going to the bank. His instructions were so clear and concise. I never saw Mr. Brown after that night; his words of wisdom worked for me. I build my duplex without ever going to the bank for a loan.

My third child was about one year old when I was getting ready to move to my new home, rent, and mortgage-free.

I knew I was not taking Donald with me, even though we were engaged to be married. We had gone through so many disagreements and invalid arguments in front of my kids. He was barely helping with the bills at the apartment; when he did come home, it was maybe a few nights a week. He would devour most of the food and drinks in the house, never replenishing them. When I did get some money from him, it was because I had to force it out of him.

My life of clubbing and drinking had escalated even to a higher level. I was now holding parties at my apartment on the weekends after I dropped my kids off at my parent's house.

My lifestyle began to affect my work ethics; I was now drinking on the job and swearing at employee meetings. My boss, whom I loved, and who I know loved me, decided to terminate me. I was nonchalant about it because I knew I deserved it; he was good to me. I could have gotten anything from him; it was him that helped pay for the foundation to my home to get dug. How can I be upset? I brought it upon myself.

When the Bible said God reigns on the just and the unjust, I know it to be real. You see, immediately after I finished building one side of my apartments getting ready to move in, I got terminated. I want to stop right here to give God praise, even though this happened a long time ago. He is still so worthy of being praised. He sent an angel, so I did not have a mortgage, then he allowed me to complete my living abode before being terminated; no one can convince me that God is not good. You may be in a season where your marriage or relationship is rocky, and it looks like all hope is lost. I want you to reflect on all God has done, you could have been dead, or strung out on drugs or contracted the aids virus, but you survived what others did not. Let us take a SELAH...........

I am sorry I'm supposed to be writing my story, but my mind goes back to this day because I still didn't give my life to Christ even though I knew it was him pulling me through. I just must praise him. God is so faithful (with tears running down my face) know that He's got you, nothing can harm you, this light affliction is only temporary. When you get out of this, you will be so grateful for how the porter made you over again.

When the time came for me to move into my house, I broke it off with Donald; I had experienced too many lies and betrayals. His mother never seemed to see my side of the story; her son was always right. He begged me not to leave him, but my mind was set on going. The problems I had had before in my past relationships had made me a little stronger and wiser.

Donald was not too pleased about my decision; he had secretly told everyone that the house was his, and he built it. Let me tell you, God, he is a keeper. When my home was being constructed, Donald would keep my car during the day because he worked at night. There were times when the builders needed materials, and he would purchase them. I now know it was God placing it in my spirit to return his money immediately, which I did each time, not knowing what was ahead.

Donald decided to make my life a living hell since I would not marry him. He would show up with his police friends bragging about the house and the car he "bought." One day one of his friends looked on the windshield of my car and saw my name on it. He whispered to himself; I thought this was Donald's car and house. I asked what he said; he responded by saying nothing. His mother and sister became angry with me because he told them he put all his money into the house, and I kicked him out. I explained to them it was false, but by then, our relationship had gone sour. One night while I was in the bar room with my friends. One of them introduced me to Bobby. He was a married man whom I grew to love dearly. It was not planned, it just happened at the bar, of course, right. Still finding men at the bars or clubs, some people never learn. I want you to stop, put the book down and think about where you are now whether you are in a relationship or not. Are you indeed where you need to be right now? Is your relationship with God healthy? Are you in an evil cycle? Listen to me; God can change your story today if you give him full access in your life. You do not have to continue that path; help is here.

Bobby was a man of sorrow; his wife was mistreating him. This woman had a good man but showed no appreciation for her provider, priest, and protector. We became close quickly; we were each other's comfort in the time of our grief. Donald was always a nuisance to me; he was not giving up easily. Wherever we went out, he would find me, flattened my tires, or break my windshield. This happened like on four to five different occasions. I knew it was him, when I approached him about it he admitted to it. Calling the Police Department was a dead end; they were his friends. Bobby was a great support, even though he was living home with his wife. We found time to be together, frequently. We were drawn together like a magnet, but he belonged to someone else, I was feeling convictions.

Bobby, one day, made up his mind to move out of his marital home to be with me. I was happy and sad at the same time because I never wanted to be in a relationship with someone's husband. I loved him; the first time I could say I was in love with a man. He was my best friend, calm, relaxed, and collective; he was educated and had dreams of his own he wanted to achieve. Bobby lived with me but still sweetheart his wife from time to time. I found out one day when he was dropping me off to work; she approached us as I was kissing him. Bobby, she said," I refuse to be your sweetheart, when I'm your wife, let me know now if you want to be with Sherry or me (that was short for Sherilyn)." Bobby, without hesitation, responded," Sherry." I did not say anything because this was her husband, and she had every right. That evening we spoke about the event that happened that day, he told me the full story and apologized to me for deceiving me. One thing I love about Bobby he would confess all he did, and seek to reconcile.

Bobby had filed for divorce, he wanted to marry me, I should have been ecstatic, but I was not because of the guilt of having another woman's husband. He insisted on marrying me, even when I spoke with him several times. God had a purpose for my life, and that was not part of it. He soon found out his wife contested the divorce because she still loved him. I remember after hearing that I sat down for literally two hours trying to convince Bobby to go back home, not because I wanted him too, but the convictions were becoming more potent. He listened and repeated, "I love you, Sherry, and I'm going to marry you." Now maybe if it were someone else, you would have rejoiced and fought to get married to this man, but I didn't. Instead of being happy for finally having someone in my life who felt the same way about me, and I felt about him, I was depressed. Donald and I always remained in contact with one another because of our daughter, and we were friends. I decided one night to go out with Donald, hoping this would do the trick, and he would move back home. But Lord, I love him so much why are you trying to take him away from me? The only man who ever loved me, I was so confused. Bobby lived with me for about ten months, and I did not get pregnant. We never practice safe sex, and back then, if you looked at me too hard, I would become pregnant. Even though I wanted Bobby to be a part of my journey, God knew he couldn't allow it or leave a seed of his with me. We would be inseparable, and eventually, I would not have cared about his wife and become a product of breaking a home permanently.

Bobby was hurt that I went out with Donald because all I went through in my relationship with Donald. I was still communicating with him. As I was riding the local transit belonging to Donald, I saw my car parked in front of a restaurant. I asked to stop so that I could get off the bus. I went inside the restaurant only to see my beloved Bobby sitting there with a woman. He was not surprised by seeing me; it was as if he planned it. The first words came out of his mouth we're," now you see how it feels." I asked him for my keys; he refused to give it to me. Donald capitalized on this opportunity and began to fight him in the restaurant. The fight eventually moved to the streets; I was embarrassed because of what was happening. I felt sorry about what was happening to the love of my life. Bobby went home that day, shattered and broken. We remained friends, and he would still call me, he wanted to come by on weekends to even help out with my business. I advised him that that was not a good idea, think about how his wife would feel. He agreed; eventually, our relationship just faded away. I thought about him all the time but knew I did the right thing.

One night while out with my friends, I had an urgency to call Bobby's wife to apologize to her. When she came home, I apologized to her for having a relationship with her husband. She began to raise her voice and stated," you took my husband away from me for ten months. I agreed with her and added, at least, I'm apologizing. She became silent, listened, and thanked me. That was the last they heard from me.

Donald was still trying to get back together with me; I couldn't trust someone who was regularly doing things to hurt me.

It was on the weekend; he asked me if I could pick our daughter from his mom's house, it was a trap set for me. While sitting on the couch, talking with his mother, he came out and kneeled, begging for me to give him a second chance. I simply replied," no." At one point, tears were streaming down his face as he begged and begged me to accept him back, I remained adamant about my answer. I felt terrible that I had to reject him in front of his mother.

One fateful night, Donald asked me if he could come over; he needed to talk to me about something extraordinarily meaningful. I am a very forgiving person, so I obliged him. My kids were in the living room, so he asked if we could talk in the room. He convinced me to have sex with him, even though I wasn't interested at the time. Donald and I were intimate from time to time; we had a love-hate relationship. I was not upset with him, just tired; he asked me if I was angry and started to apologize. I was so numb I did not even respond. A month later, I found out I was pregnant with my first son; at this point, I wanted to die. I at least wanted to be settled down before having a next child. It seemed my life would never get any better.

Prayer points for grace and mercy

Psalm 51:1-2, O Lord, have mercy on me and blot out all my sins, in the name of Jesus.

Ephesians 2:4-5, O Lord, because of Your love and compassion over me, save me by Your grace so that I will be worthy of your blessings, in the name of Jesus.

Psalm 25:6-7/James 2:13; O God of Mercy, do not remember the iniquities of my past to judge me, remember me today and tonight, in the name of Jesus.

Hebrew 4: 16; O God, I come before You today to obtain mercy and find grace to fulfill my purpose, in the name of Jesus.

Matthew 6:7; O Lord, I receive Your grace to have mercy upon this person............... (Mention name), in the name of Jesus.

Genesis 39:21; Just as the way you were with Joseph and showed him steadfast love and favor in the sight of the keeper of the prison, By Your Mercy O Lord, let the proportion of Joseph's blessings reach me, in the name of Jesus.

Romans 9:18; O God of Joseph, arise and show me in Your loving mercy, in the name of Jesus.

Lam 3:17; Any evil from the mouth of men against my life, Mercy of God, cancel them, in the name of Jesus.

1 Cor 3:17; Anything in my life serving as a defilement of my body and spiritual life, die, in the name of Jesus.

Romans 10:9; By Your great Hand of Mercy, raise me up from these sins (Mention them) and save me, in the name of Jesus.

Matthew 6:33; I receive the grace to seek after Your kingdom and righteousness alone so that everything I am looking for shall be added unto me, in the name of Jesus.

Isaiah 53:6; O Lord, If I have gone astray, If I have been disconnected from the power of Your Salvation, let Your grace bring me back, in the name of Jesus.

Matthew 24:35, For it is written that Heaven and earth shall pass away, but Your words in my heart shall not pass away, it shall stay to bring greater results for me, in the name of Jesus.

Gal 5:19-21; Any secret sins I am harboring that is not blessing my life, I decree they shall be destroyed, in the name of Jesus.

At the bus stop of disappointment, Mercy of God, bail me out, in the name of Jesus.

I frustrate any power pushing me away from enjoying the great mercy of God, in the name of Jesus.

The mercy of God lifts me above my present situations in the name of Jesus' name.

O God of Daniel, hear my cry of mercy, in the name of Jesus.

Oh, Son of David, let today be the beginning of my total freedom, in the name of Jesus.

O Lord, if I am not permitted to be one of the candidates of heaven, Mercy of God, push me there, in the name of Jesus.

Premarital Counseling Questionnaire

Below are some questions that can be used in your time or at a Women's Fellowship. We must do a deep soul searching before we say I do.

17. Should each of you be permitted one night a week for your own interests?

_____

18. Do you think that certain dates (anniversary, birthdays, etc.) should be remembered by your mate?

_____

19. Has divorce occurred in your family?

_____

*20. Do you plan to live with your family or your mate's family?*_____

21. What is your thinking regarding the matter of "in-laws"?

_____

Chapter 4

Desperate for love

After my termination, I started selling food and alcohol from home. The Holy Spirit was convicting me to stop selling alcoholic beverages; as a result, my sales went down. I began looking for employment to sustain my children and I. After my baby boy was born, I decided to rededicate my life to Christ. I decided to stay away from Donald completely; he was terrible for me. I started to attend a local church in my area. Anytime I begin to participate in a church, I would almost immediately be given assignments, I was never sat down or counseled. This happens mostly in smaller ministries. Sometimes Pastors could become desperate to find people to fill ministry positions. We ought to discipline a person first, get to know them before putting them in critical situations. I had not received training in any of the ministries I was appointed to work. I was at this church barely a month, and already,

72

I was helping with the Christmas production, something I love even to this day. One night after practice, the preacher got up and began bashing me indirectly about my dress being too short and accusing me of being seductive. I was dumbfounded; my joy ended quickly. The church is a hospital for all; I should feel safe and loved there. Even if he thought it was true, sit me down and talk to me as a father. Satan was happy; he started talking again, "see I would never treat you like that; go get a drink to forget about the church." I never went back to that church; I decided to take the devil's advice, drinking, and clubbing again. I met Kenneth at the bar where I hung out with my friends. I met Kenneth a year after my son was born. Kenneth was a year younger than I, very handsome and tall. We started casually talking about life while we were having drinks. He asked me for my number, which I gave to him; I thought he was too young for me. I was uncomfortable with the idea of dating someone a year younger than I.

We started talking every day, meeting up to hang out frequently. I knew deep down he was not the one, but I felt I had to try, maybe this time it will work. I started to attend the church where I grew up; I was still being convicted, although I was making bad choices. Kenneth began to attending church with me; this was a good sign. We soon started talking about getting married. His uncle was a preacher who did not believe in divorce; he told him not to marry me. I wanted to be a happily married woman until I was obsessed. I felt hurt and rejected, but I knew he was right about him not marrying me. This is the first time I prayed about my relationship. I asked God to show me a sign if we should get married or not. Some of you reading this book have prayed the same thing, knowing the answer. We can be blinded by our desire to get married for our selfish desires. One night after coming from the club, we got into a huge argument. I don't remember what the case was about, but it was intense. I stopped the car and told him to get out and never come back. He agreed with me, swearing, he slammed the door, and I sped off.

God had answered my prayers, yes, Lord. Two days later, I called him, asking him to come over, wanting to reconcile our differences. He came over, so we could talk and clear the air.

I initially met his mother and grandparents, who were ok with our relationship. There were still so many signs telling me not to go any further. I, as usual, didn't pay attention to any of the posters.

A few months later, we decided to live together. This, of course, is not a good idea on any level. God designed a couple to live together after marriage. Many couples make the mistake of living like they were married. Some end up never getting married or separated. Marriage is a covenant ordained by God. A woman should only move in with her husband under that covenant. Sin is sweet but always ends with a bitter taste. The word of God can't lie, the Bible declares in Romans 6:23" the wages of sin is death." The enemy will always try to make you feel comfortable in sin; we convince ourselves that it is ok God understands.

We lived together for about a year before we got married. I was against us just shacking (living together unmarried) up, so I posed the question to him a few times "when are we getting married?" He was all for getting married and seemed excited as I was. We made plans to get married at a church with just the JP. My mom was the only one present, as most of his family was against it. He had no support from his side of the family. Who cares, we're not marrying our families, so I thought. This is far from the truth when you marry someone; you marry the entire family. They can be a blessing or a curse depending on how well you get along with them.

This was now my second marriage; I felt there was hope. Ladies, it is essential to take time to get to know someone. Make sure to take the person to your Pastor; they watch over your soul. Do not allow your emotions to cloud your thinking; see a person for who they are. Don't deny what you see; signs are always there, we just don't pay attention to them. Waiting on God's timing is far better than going through unnecessary suffering. God's timing is the best. There is a man out there for you, let him find you.

I had stopped selling food from my house; I gained employment at an Insurance Company as a sales agent. Kenneth worked for the government doing maintenance such as painting, road paving, just to name a few. He hated being on that job. He hoped to one day leave and start his own business.

Weeks after we got married, Kenneth decided to quit his job to stay at home. My house had great amenities, such as central air, direct tv, internet, and computer. Most homes in third world countries lack most of these amenities. I felt hurt that he would want to stay home, play games, and watch tv. I came back from work every day, noticing he was becoming more comfortable at home. I decided to approach him, asking him if he thought my house was "Sherry's Motel." You need to get a job as soon as possible, no grown man going to stay at home while I work. The devil is a liar. When he quit the Government job, his boss was still paying him every month, in case he wanted to return. We were not sure when the money would stop coming. We learned later that his boss had made that arrangement for him. I was still not satisfied because he did not work in or outside the home. He made my two older daughters do a lot of chores. I passionately believe if one spouse is at home all day, he/she should take care of the house by cooking and cleaning. One night, I stepped in and asked him not to keep my kids up late to do housework when he is at home every day.

After weeks of pestering him, Kenneth got another job, doing the same type of work he was doing at his previous position. I was glad he was working and out of the house.

My joy was short-lived; he came home from the first day, complaining about how he did not like the job he was on. I believed he just did not want to work. He felt he struck gold, a desperate woman with four children; she will take care of me. There are a lot of young men out there with intentions of marrying an older or desperate woman in hopes of having a comfortable life. He even stopped going to church with me and the kids, he was finally displaying who he was. We argued almost every day about him not wanting to work. He quit the job and did not tell me until I noticed he was home again every day. Don't get me wrong; by this time, I was an angry black woman, tired of being used and abused. Kenneth once referred to me as a ticking time bomb. I was vicious in an argument; my words could cut you like a sword when I was angry.

I was the proud mother of four when Kenneth and I got married. I got pregnant with my fifth child about a year after we were married. I was extremely sick with this pregnancy and couldn't function at work. My boss had me ride along with another agent who collected from my clients on my behalf. Wherever I went, I always gave one hundred percent on my job. I was the same way in my relationships; I was in one hundred percent.

Kenneth had found another job, doing electrical work. He seemed to like the job he was on. We were growing apart daily, and we could not see eye to eye. We were always in arguments. One night while disagreeing, we were in the room; he slapped me lightly. He caught himself quickly and apologized, that didn't stop me from going wild. I began shouting and screaming, reminding him I was an independent black woman. Then these words came out of his mouth" you should be glad someone wants to marry a woman with four children." Those words confirmed to me his actions for quitting all his jobs. What is in someone's heart will eventually come out. He saw my desperation; wow, I should have been crushed by those words, but I wasn't. I made up in my mind that day. I was utterly giving my life to Christ. Our marriage had gotten toxic; it was beyond repair at this time. Let me advise you about reading this book; it is essential to receive counseling before and during your marriage. The Bible says in *Proverbs 15:22,"* *Where there is no counsel, plans fail, but in a multitude* *of counselors, they are established."*

One Mother's Day, I came home from church to an empty house. Kenneth was gone. My first husband did the same thing, walked out while I was so pregnant, I could barely function when I got inside. I went into the room laid down immediately; I felt I was about to faint what he did affect my children, especially my oldest daughter. They had grown fond of him; he would help the kids with their homework. He was good with the children. He was helping my daughter study for her BJC's (examination like FSA). My oldest daughter could not focus when she took her exams; she didn't perform very well. She was devastated, as was I.

I was seven and a half months pregnant with our daughter. Kenneth never called me once to find out if I was okay. I was left to wallow in my sorrow. I am a good person, why does this keep happening to me? What was I doing wrong? I was driving to the grocery store when a voice told me just to kill myself. I agreed briefly to the thought of harming myself before I thought about my children, whom I loved so much, and quickly dismissed the thoughts. I struggled with depression and suicidal thoughts every day. I cried myself to sleep every night. I cannot allow this innocent child to be born under these circumstances.

I inquired with one of my agent friends as to where I could go to get an abortion. I could not keep this child; I was going insane. Miraculously I had stopped drinking and clubbing for a good while. I wanted to go back to that old lifestyle, but something would not allow me too. I know

now it was the Holy Spirit. She made an appointment for me to talk about the pregnancy. We were getting ready to go to the clinic when a firm conviction came upon me. I told my friend I could not go through with it; she was furious and called me stupid. I felt stupid, but I obeyed the voice of the Holy Spirit.

On July 5th, I gave birth to a beautiful baby girl. I called Kenneth to inform him about the child's birth. He was happy to hear the news; he came over later that day to see her.

My relationship with God was volatile; I knew I wanted to remain with God. My mother's church was not helping me to grow spiritually, so I left and was attending another church in the church of God denomination. I loved the new church I attended; it was livelier and filled with youth. There was a man in the church whom I had gotten close to, not sexually just a platonic relationship. He was teaching me the word of God; I had so many questions being a new convert. While I was curious about God and his word, I also wanted to have greater intimacy with God. My husband and I were on good terms again; he wanted to make our marriage work. He was coming around to see the kids and spend time, or I would go to his place. I spoke with my kids about him wanting to go back home. They were not in agreement, especially my oldest daughter. She told me if I ever got back with him, she would never forgive me. I understood they were hurt. Sometimes, ladies, we could be so selfish and forget about our kids and suffer in silence when we make poor decisions. I put my kids so through so much chasing after marriage, which is not ok. God has put in his word what is required of a man and woman during the marriage. No one tried to give me godly counsel, nor did I know to look for counsel. My poor mom just wanted her children married and doing well.

I spoke with who I would call my mentor about my husband's intention; he told me not to make it easy for him.

He thought it was good he wanted to work on the marriage, but he wanted me to be sure I was making the right decision. Kenneth did not seem sincere with his requests. Maybe he felt guilty about how he treated me. I prayed about it and decided to take it slow if we were to reunite. I was so caught up in my newfound relationship with Christ; I did not want to make any mistakes. Eventually, Kenneth and I grew apart; he was still into clubbing and drinking. I needed a change; I was going around in cycles. We decided to go our separate ways.

My mentor and I became close. We would be on the phone for hours talking about the Lord. I would even call him each time the baby got up in the night, he was happy to keep my company. I was used to having male friends, so I was not trying to get into a relationship with him. He had a girlfriend he was talking to and wanted to marry. My relationship with God was growing. I was experiencing joy and peace. I had given up that lifestyle of clubbing and drinking. I had found a love like no other, praise the Lord. Let me encourage you; whether you are married or thinking of marriage, it's not too late to allow God to be the center of your relationship. A lot of times, we feel we know better than God does, not understanding the earth and everything in it belongs to Him. God wants the best for us and desires to see and in good health and prosper even as our soul prospers. (3 John 1:3)

Lord to make me over again; I need your guidance, my story must change.

Prayer points against rejection

I repent of my self-righteousness and where I have rejected those in the church and not obeyed Your command of love of the brethren and acceptance of the beloved and not walking in love.

I repent also where I have justified my own rebellion and disobedience to Your Word and ways because of a stronghold of the transgression of pride.

I also repent of my pride in prosperity, my furniture, my belongings, my car, my income, my business, my career, and even my calling and position in the church.

I repent the pride of my heritage, my ancestry, my parent's lineage, and achievements and even where they have instilled in me pride because of all this.

Lord Jesus, I repent of my hardness of heart and my stony heart because of all my pride. I repent where I have refused subjection and dependence upon you because of my rebellious pride. I repent where I have given honor and glory to myself instead of You because of my pride.

I repent of all mockery and scorn and foolishness, my proud looks of contempt and haughtiness, and a proud heart. I repent of all disrespect, dishonor to parents and elders, and disrespect for authority with arrogance and all lying. I repent of envy, shame, strife, blasphemy, and arguing.

I repent of all greed, gluttony, slothfulness, idleness and all sexual sins of lust and those committed in drunkenness. I repent where I have compromised Your

Word with Your instruction not to sin, to live righteously, and for where I have compromised Your Word to follow after the lusts of the flesh and the ways of the world.

Lord Jesus, I ask you to bring to death the sin structures of all my pride, stubbornness, and rebellion.

Oh Lord, cause me to realize that I am to live a life of humility in agreement with You to love crucified in this area of my life.

Oh lord, Enable me to realize that the old man has to die and that I am to live in newness of life as You continue to do a work within my heart.

I repent and renounce all fascination with the forbidden and even the supernatural.

I repent where I have unknowingly allowed this stronghold of pride to counterfeit my life and the works and manifestations of Your Holy Spirit.

I ask for a loosing of my ears and eyes and tongue so I can hear and see and speak to move in Your Holy Spirit.

Father where I have opened myself up to false tongues because of pride and any other religious spirits or evil spirits from the laying on of hands.

Father, I ask for the deliverance of all these spirits that have entered into me.

Father where I may have any of these specific spirits of pride: "Foot of Pride (Psalm 26:11); Rod of Pride (Proverbs 14:3); Crown of Pride (Isaiah 28:1, 3); Great

Pride (Jeremiah 13:9); Pride of Life (1 John 2:16)." I claim the children's bread of deliverance of demons.

Premarital Counseling Questionnaire

Below are some questions that can be used in your time or at a Women's Fellowship. We must do a deep soul searching before we say I do.

22. How many children would you like to have?

_____

23. Who is to be the head of your home?

_____

24. What is your plan for settling family problems?

_____

25. Who is to exercise the discipline of children?

_____

26. Should your mate ever keep anything a secret from you? If so, what?

_____

27. Is the wife in this family going to work?

_____

Chapter 5

God told me to marry you

Wilfred (my mentor) and I started talking for hours on the phone about the Bible. He was truly knowledgeable about the Bible. I would ask him questions after questions. I was so hungry for knowledge and wanted to know every detail about God. We soon became inseparable; we went everywhere together. I was still working at the insurance job. One thing I disagree with was having to collect insurance in the evenings,

He would accompany me to see my clients because it could be hazardous for collecting money in the neighborhoods where I went. We had to collect money from our clients every week. The area I was assigned to was high in crimes; it got challenging in the evenings, especially when the time changed in October. I loved my children and wanted the best for them, so I endured. Wilfred, he was a good friend to me, a breath of fresh air. I thanked God for him being in

91

my life. I do not know how I would have made it without him.

At this point in my life, I had asked God to please help me to become celibate; I just wanted to work for him. I prayed day and night, asking God to use me. I just wanted to be focused on Him and Him alone. I concluded marriage was not for me. Love was not for me; I am destined to be a woman of sorrow.

Insurance pays very well if you work hard. I was torn up inside about my past life, and all that had happened, that my performance was minimal. I was slowly losing my desire for my job. I was slowly losing passion for everything, even life itself. Why was I ever born? What is the purpose? I'm sure many of you are reading this book have asked these questions. Never doubt it, you have a purpose, and you matter more than you know. Life may not be the way you dreamt it, and it seems all hope is lost, but it is not. That is a trick from the enemy, and sometimes, the inner me (you) can be an enemy to us as well. I needed a change, so I took a second job at Lickety Split, I wanted to have a less demanding job and a new beginning. I remember Wilfred coming there to visit me sometimes; the workers thought he was my husband or boyfriend. I asked him to stop calling me on my job because of the comments people we're making. I had already made up in my mind to be alone for the rest of my life. He continued to come, despite my disapproval. He was a good friend to me.

The church where Wilfred and I attended was a small church, which his father was the Pastor. My kids and I started to become active at church. I found this church after asking my mom to suggest a church for us to attend.

After attending there for some months, the members saw that Wilfred and I were becoming close, many of them despised our friendship. They thought I was seducing him into being with me because they knew my husband had left. People were making unhealthy remarks while I walked past, sometimes they would stop me to ask about my involvement with Wilfred.

I was furious, that was not on my mind, no one asked me how I was managing or holding up since my husband left. My baby girl was maybe eight to nine months old. I was a wounded soldier, bleeding right in the pew. What good would a man do for me at this time? I was not pursuing him, he sought me, but of course, I looked desperate to people. Wilfred would always be the one to call and check up on me to see how I was doing; I took it for just that. Church folks have a way to condemn a person already feeling ashamed and guilty. People look from natural eyes rather than see a person through the eye of the Holy Spirit. Many people walk out of the church doors never to return because of the way they are judged and ridiculed at church. Many suicide and murders or other casualties can be avoided if the church of Jesus Christ discern what people are going through and offer a solution. Most people are looking for answers; they need a savior. Sometimes we see a broken vessel that in the eyesight of people is beyond repair. You, reading this book, remember God has the last say so. You are not defined by man's opinion. God already gives a fact about your life.

Psalms 139:14

I will praise You, for [a]I am fearfully and wonderfully made;

Marvelous are Your works, And that my soul knows very well.

After a long day of riding around collecting insurance premiums, I was headed to drop Wilfred home. When I pulled up in the yard, I noticed there were boxes outside on the ground. He got out of the car and realized that his brother had put all his belongings outside. He tried opening the door but soon realized they had changed the lock. He looked startled and hurt, but he never said a word. He bought his belongings and jumped back in my car. What are you going to do? I asked. He was quiet for a few moments; I could feel he was very hurt by what his brother had done. How could you put your brother out without even an explanation as to why? He was not coming in all hours of the morning or being a burden to his brother. I guess that his story and we will never know why.

Wilfred's father was not close to any of his kids; he was swamped as most pastors are. A lot of times, Pastors neglect their families and focus on others. His father was not a pleasant man, and his mom had mild dementia. His brothers were doing well for themselves, all married with children and promising careers.

He was not welcomed at his father's house, for reasons I don't know. The only reasonable choice was to take him home with me. When we got to the house, I showed him to my room and told him I would sleep in my daughter's room. I was ok with this because after all, he had a fiancé he was getting married to, so he wouldn't be here long.

Wilfred and I began to pray and read the Bible daily; my faith was growing in God. He was sharing the word of God with me and helping me to understand my walk with God.

Wilfred saw my zeal and desire for God was so sincere; he realized I needed more guidance than he could offer. He introduced me to a mighty woman of God, a Prophetess, a woman of prayer. It was hard for me at first to accept talking to anyone, because of all the rejection I had already experienced in life. I never opened to anyone the way I did with Wilfred; It was effortless to have a conversation with him. I never had female friends or mentors in my life up to this point; even now, I do not have any female friends. That is a whole different story for another book, miss curious. Let us continue our story, shall we?

Prophetess Deborah had an immensely powerful prayer ministry, which Wilfred attended.

We started to attend the prayer meeting every Thursday at faithfully. This was all new for me, even though I grew up in church, I stopped attending when I was in my late teens after my first pregnancy. I now had five children, with a whole lot of other baggage.

I loved the atmosphere and what I felt each time I attended the Prayer meetings. I began to participate in the Monday night prayer meeting as well, my hunger and thirst for God were like the Psalmist declared " as the Deer panteth after the waters so my soul longest after thee" The joy I felt was unexplainable!

I decided after some time to make weekly appointments to see Prophetess Deborah, to discuss my walk with God, and understand ministry. She was very patient and kind; she became easy to talk to after a period. Wilfred played the keyboard faithfully for the Thursday's Prayer Meetings, hosted by Prophetess Deborah. Did I mention he played the keyboard? He was exceptionally good at it when he played; you would get lost in the presence of God. One day he suggested that I do the opening song for the Meetings. I was so afraid; I could not sing in front of people. My heart started to race at a pace that almost knocked the wind out of me. After speaking with Prophetess again on the matter, I decided to give it a try. I love to sing but did not think I was good enough to sing in front of a crowd. After leading worship, for a while, I became more confident doing the work of the Lord.

Over the months after seeking God in prayer, I had decided to resign my job as an Insurance Agent. I believe God was calling me unto himself, to work in his vineyard.

I was still working at Lickety Split; they wanted me to become the manager there. I was grateful for the offer, but I know that position was not for me. I was waiting for the right time to leave.

I dreamt one night that God was saying to me, Wilfred was my husband. I immediately began a fast because I honestly believed that the devil was trying to distract me. I remember going into the bathroom at work and crying out to God to save me and from this distraction. You see, as the songwriter wrote," I had found a love that pardons, had found some stripes that heal, I had found strength for my weakness and had found grace to cove cover all my sins in Jesus." I told Wilfred, about what I believed God was showing me, I always told him everything that I dream or my encounters with God. I went on further to say, that is impossible, hoping he would agree. He said to me calmly, "woman of God, I'm going on a fast, and I will speak with you after." ok, as I shrugged my shoulder, I had no idea what his fasting was concerning.

After his time away in fasting, Wilfred came up to pick me up from work one day, so I quickly ran out to meet him. I was still being protective of people thinking he was my boyfriend or husband. Wilfred was a very handsome, tall, and dark man; a lot of women were attracted to him. He had women throwing themselves at him; we would laugh about it after service. Why on earth would a man of his caliber want to marry me, when Wilfred could have any woman he wanted. When I got in the car, he was quiet. I was curious as to why but didn't ask. He said to me a few moments later, can I have some of your ice creams, please? I was puzzled; the only words I could have found were I licked all over this. He was insistent, so I gave it to him, still confused. Shortly after eating my ice cream, he spoke to me what God had said to him. God wanted him to marry me. What? Wait! That's not the answer I was looking for, God why?

. I had to digest what he said to me; it was troubling me. I made an appointment with the Prophetess. This man had gone mad, were my thoughts. To my despair, she confirmed what I feared; he was my husband. After a few weeks, I quit the job at Lickety Split, to be in full-time ministry for the Lord.

Wilfred and I already had a great friendship. It was still hard to transition to a committed relationship. As we were talking, one night, he admitted to me that after we started talking on the phone, his desire to speak with his fiancé grew less. He told her of our relationship, and she was ok with it. He told me he was praying to God for a wife, but he pleaded with her in mind. The Holy Spirit shouted out to him, ok, take her as your wife. God was giving him his permissive will because that's what he wanted. I was having a difficult time believing he could ever love me as his wife.

We wanted a fresh start because his father's church became very toxic to our relationship. One of the pastors he was playing for on Sunday mornings was where we decided to attend. A few weeks after attending there, my Pastor asked to lead Praise and Worship on Sunday mornings. I helped to lead ministries wherever I attended almost immediately. I was excited to do whatever I could find to do in the house of God. I still needed guidance and discipleship.

Mother Sally, we called her, was an extraordinary lady, she gravitated to me almost immediately. After a period, she had a meeting with us about our relationship, wanting to know when we were going to get married.

She said that people were saying Wilfred had degraded, they couldn't believe he could be in a relationship with someone like me, much less marry me. There was so much negative energy from both sides of our families. My mother came to my house one day, stating she needed to pray for me. She followed me into the room where Wilfred was. She started praying immediately she got into my room, asking God to remove the snake (my husband to be) from around my legs. We had a big laugh that night over the prayer. It seemed everyone was against us, but we remained focused on what God had requested from us.

We told Mother Sally about the challenge we faced. I was trying to get my divorce. Mother Sally gave the remaining balance to me to pay the lawyer to finalize my divorce.

After some months, I finally was free to get married to Wilfred. We got married in a Pastor's office with only two witnesses.

Our life was going well; we took part in a few ministries at our local church. My husband and I traveled to many places to minister and sing, or sometimes it was just him alone playing for a ministry. We wanted to follow God and faithfully obey all he asked us to do. I had gotten pregnant before we got married, so I had my son shortly after we got married. The only person that came to visit our son and us was his sister Shantel. She was supportive of our relationship and marriage. She wanted to take my baby to visit his grandfather. When she got back, she told me she rested the baby on his lap for him to hold him; he did not attempt to reach for the baby. My baby began to fall from his lap; he remained with his arm folded; she had to run to catch my baby from falling. I was hurt hearing such cruelty to an innocent child; he was a very cold-hearted man.

He wanted nothing to do with either of us; he was not in agreement with our relationship or marriage. My husband decided to visit his father to have a word with him about the way he was treating him. He also wanted to let him know we were transitioning to another church. I was anticipating a negative report on his return from his father. I was anxiously waited for my husband to return. He finally got home; I couldn't wait for him to get inside the house before the questions started.

"Hold on a minute, woman," he said, "at least let me change my clothes and relax a bit."

"Okay, honey, I'll wait until you're ready," I responded. Later that evening, he told me the conversation between his father and himself was pointless. He had approached him about his lack of support for our marriage. His father yelled out angrily, "why did you marry that lady, with all those kids?'. He told him, "God told me to marry her.' This sounds like a great answer, but months later, I got the revelation to what he had meant. People were in his ears, repeatedly telling him about the mistake he had made in marrying me. It started to take a toll on him; it began to show. He began to scorn me; he looked at me in disgust. I guess the words of the people were weakening his love for me and what God had told him. When we went out, he would find reasons to ensure he's not seated next to me. On one occasion, we were at a Tent Crusade. He sat next to me briefly. Just as he was getting up, I asked, "why do you always find a reason not to sit with me, are you embarrassed?' He mumbled something under his breath and proceeded to leave anyway. I would regularly ask for us to go on dates; he refused each time. I realized he was ashamed of being with me. On a Valentine night, we went on a boat cruise for spouses, he sat away from me, even though he saw me shivering from the cold. Everyone else was cuddling and enjoying themselves; he ignored me the entire night. Then the sentence became alive to me, 'God told me to marry you.' My husband was used to what we called "mango skin" women. These were light-skinned women who were very extravagant in their appearance. I was not as fortunate as they were to adorn myself so extravagantly. We were in full-time ministry, so we depended solely on God's provision. Life became challenging at times, having to feed the kids and take care of the basic needs of the house. I encouraged him to try to get a part-time job instead of sleeping late in the day. I believe a man should do his best to provide for his family above all odds. Passionately I think no person should be sleeping so late if they are going to succeed in life. Wilfred has had a series of women in his life who pampered him and gave him what he wanted. Married women, single women all flocked to his side, ready to do his bidding. He loved that I was different and challenged him to become better than just using his charms to retrieve what he wanted. There were a few occasions I was packing his clothes for him to leave my house. Wilfred and my relationship started to decline intensely. That sweet communication we had was no more, we barely spoke. I was devastated. I didn't want to live like this anymore. Each time I asked him to leave, he would tell me not to send him away and that he needed me. I am not sure if he meant it, or it was just because he had nowhere to go.

We were still very faithful to the Prayer Ministry on Thursday afternoons. Wilfred had stopped going to the Monday night prayer meetings, for reasons I would learn later. I asked him a few times why and he would not tell me until one day he gave in. 'The truth is I was lusting at Prophetess Sharon; I can't take my eyes off her bust". I laughed loudly; he was shocked at my response. He made me promise not to tell her he would confess himself. That is the kind of relationship we had; we were able to tell each other about anything. I thanked him for telling me and offered to help him through it. My husband was very promiscuous before he gave his life to Christ. It seems he was still struggling with his addictions. He started to behave strangely in front of me. Sometimes kissing a woman on her cheeks. When I approached him, he responded, "I don't see anything wrong with kissing a sister in Christ." You see, this young lady was the type of woman he craved; she was a mango skin. He did this in front of me on several occasions. I was never upset or jealous; I never felt he belonged to me; I did not think I was good enough.

My spiritual life grew in leaps and bounds; God was truly empowering me and filling me with his Holy Spirit. At one point, he became jealous of the way God was using me. He admitted it after I felt it in my spirit and confronted him. He wanted to know why God was using me, and he taught me all I know. To further his frustrations, people would bless us, but they would always give me the finances or bring new clothing for me. One day he blurted out, "they don't see I need d____ clothes as well, my shoe heels are falling off. I tried to console him the best way I could.

I felt very alone and rejected in this marriage. My insecurities were at a significant high; I did not understand why God would put me through this when I told him I was not interested in having a husband. My only joy was spending time with Jesus; I found peace and joy in his presence. I prayed to God, telling him I would endure whatever pain or hardship he wanted me to go through. I would have remained married to Wilfred even though I was unhappy.

Wilfred and I got some counseling from our leader, we both agreed to try after some time of us just not communicating. Wilfred had a lot of photos of women from his past relationships. I told him he needed to get rid of them so that we could have a fresh start. He agreed and did just that. Things started to get better between us; he was trying to communicate as best as he could. We would spend hours reading and studying the word of God together.

Wow, he said I remember when you used to come to me to teach you the word, now I must come to you. I encouraged him and told him I wish I had his gift of revelation and knowledge of the word of God he had. He was not receiving my words of encouragement, each time he would repeat to me that I do not need him anymore. One day he said to me, I asked God to take me home because I don't want to be a hindrance to you. How ironic we were both praying the same prayer. The enemy had caused us to become divided instead of us complementing each other's gifts. We acknowledge where we were and hoped things would get better for us.

Time had passed, when one day Wilfred told me he had a dream, he said:" I dreamt that there was a big celebration, all my family and friends were there, but I was the only one not there." I did not comment on the dream, because I did not know what God was saying, I believe he hid it from us.

We were getting ready for a Prayer meeting one Thursday morning as usual. He said to me," guess what?" I said, what? Daddy asked me when I was coming home. This statement didn't alert me because we were planning to return to his father's church to help with ministry. His father was getting older and needed help. We had an appointment with our Pastor to inform him of our intentions.

I never knew this would be the last time we had a conversation. At prayer meeting that day, Wilfred played the keyboard like an angel, he sang as if he was around the throne of God. It was awesome; I could picture that day even now. I went home after the prayer meeting, but Wilfred had to help his father set up for a Tent Revival they were having. He got home late that night, so we did not have the opportunity to talk as we usually would before we went to bed. The next morning, I got up early because my daughter was graduating from junior high school. Wilfred stayed home with the baby and my two-year-old little girl. I woke him up to let him know I was leaving. I was about to leave when I felt a desire to kiss him goodbye. That was the last time I saw my husband alive. I was very uneasy at graduation, so I kept calling home. I got the answering machine, so I figured he was sleeping late as usual.

Graduation ended around noon; I got home around two after catching two different buses to get there. When I got to the front door, my spirit was still very uneasy. I saw a note on the door left by my pastor. We had an appointment with him to discuss leaving his church to return to his father's church to help in ministry. When I turned the door handle and noticed it was locked, I immediately knew something was wrong. We never lock the door if one of us is away. Go around the back, see if it was left open, I shouted to my daughter. She dashed along with her friend.

The door was open; she shouted from the inside as she was coming to open the door for the rest of us.

I quickly ran into the room, followed by my daughter and her friend. I was terrified as I saw my seven months old baby on the floor crying, and my two-year-old daughter was sleeping on my husband's back. I remove her gently and quickly. My husband was stuck between the nightstand and the bed. Help me get him out. I shouted at the girls. We removed the nightstand, which was being held steadfast in a corner next to a wall. The last of his breath came out of his lungs as we removed him. I did not know at the time what was happening. I called the ambulance; the attendant asked me a series of questions then asked me to administer CPR. I'm unable to get his mouth open I said; she then said, ok, just wait for the ambulance to arrive. I called my father in law. I was so devastated, he said to me," why are you telling me that your problem, not mine, he's your husband" I was stunned that even in a situation like this he remained heartless. Prophetess Sharon came to the house to console me in my time of need. The only family showing up on his side was his sister. Here I had no electricity, no food, no water and now no husband. I was left alone to struggle in this wilderness period. God had taken us through a time of famine, I lost everything, my car, and other earthly possessions, our entire dependence was on God. In these times, we saw miracles where God would speak to a person to bless us right in the nick of time.

His death was hard for me to endure. Many people called to give their condolences, even people I never knew. I was accused by some people that I was the cause of his death. I had a Pastor come to my house to tell me God told her I was a witch, and she saw my husband like an older man drying up. I told her I wish I were a lot of people who would be in trouble. What nonsense, people would say all sought of things in the name of God. Someone might have given you a prophecy about who your husband will be or when you are getting married. Sometimes false prophets play on your emotions to take advantage of you. When a true prophet gives you a prophecy you must check for a few things, does it line up with the word? Does it bring comfort? Does the person giving me the word, have the spirit of Christ?

Planning his funeral had put the icing on the cake. It seemed my pain knew no end. My pastor called me and spoke to me about the arrangements. He told me he was only going to allow me to spearhead the planning of his funeral. We had a meeting with his family to make the final plans. My Pastor opened the meeting and proceeded to direct his conversion to Wilfred's brothers. I was shocked after the conversation we had I was expecting to speak. I watched as they talked about me as if I were not there. One of his brothers boldly said," well, if she were home, maybe this would not have happened." I was silent during the entire meeting. I felt disgusted and resentment from them. My Pastor did not protect me. I felt so small at that meeting; I thought I was dreaming. I dreaded going to his funeral; I was asking God's strength through that day. Prophetess Sharon was supportive at the funeral; she was a shoulder to lean on. I laid my partner to rest on June 19th, 2004.

God, where do I go from here? Somebody, please help me.

Prayer points to prepare me for marriage

1. Thank God because He alone is the perfect matchmaker

2. Lord, release the man/woman you have preordained as my spouse in Jesus' name.

3. Lord, cause it to happen that the divine match will come forth soon in the name of Jesus.

4. Lord, let my spouse be a person who loves You wholeheartedly in the name of Jesus.

5. Lord, establish our home according to the scriptures in Jesus' name (read Ephesians 5:20-28).

6. Father, let all satanic barriers keeping us from meeting be dissolved in Jesus' name.

7. Lord, send forth your warring angels to battle and release my spouse wherever s/he is in the name of Jesus.

8. Lord, I believe You have created me for a special person; bring it to pass in the name of Jesus.

9. I now call him/her out of obscurity into my life in Jesus' name.

10. I reject the provision of a counterfeit spouse by the enemy in the name of Jesus.

11. I cut off the flow of any inherited marital problems into my life in the mighty name of Jesus (pray this one 7 times… aggressively)

12. O Lord, let the spirit of patience reign in my life until the right person comes in the name of Jesus.

Father, in the name of Jesus, just as Abraham sent his servant to find his son Isaac a wife, send the Holy Spirit to bring my future partner to me.

Thank the Lord for the answer.

Premarital Counseling Questionnaire

Below are some questions that can be used in your time or at a Women's Fellowship. We must do a deep soul searching before we say I do.

28. Are you sure that you are a child of God, having received Christ as your own Savior? If yes,

explain how you know this as fact.

_____

_____

29. Are your parents Christians?

_____

30. Can you honestly say that you believe that your mate is a Christian?

_____

31. How will you worship as a family?

_____

32. How will you grow in the faith together as husband and wife?

_____

33. Do you need some direction in the above two questions?

_____

Chapter 6

I deserve what I can get

I was given the word from the Lord that he wanted me to move to America. I concurred with the word of God; my spirit identified with it. I had many prophecies telling me about how God was going to restore everything I lost. My thoughts were, when I arrive in the USA like abracadabra, God would restore my life, give me a new partner to work within the ministry. I did not want to get married because I was desperate anymore, but because of ministry.

I met many challenges when I came to America, but God was with me. In my first book, Flawed to Masterpiece, gives you a more detailed view. I was living in Hallandale for about a year and later moved down to my present address a year later.

Prophetess Sharon had moved to the USA as well; she was in Bible College, she was also living in the area where I was. A lot of people speculated that I moved here because of her. I loved her, but not enough to make me go here.

I was attending a local church in the area. Shortly after visiting there, I promoted to the position of the youth leader. I loved my post because I love helping people. Even though I was busy, I still found myself desiring a partner. As time went by, I soon started to feel lonely; it had been four years since my husband had died. I wanted to be in a relationship because I desired to work in ministry. I started praying to God to help me find the right person; I was in excruciating loneliness. I have no family or friends in the area I lived in the area. It was difficult, at times, not having proper recreation. I found myself sinking into depression again. I love the Lord but did not know why my life was on a roller coaster. It was incredibly challenging maintaining my rent and taking care of my kids. I was crying out to God for help, but it seemed he forgot about me. I began to make poor decisions by getting involved in intimate relationships.

Lord, there must be a better way. The truth about it is if you have not asked God to help you overcome struggles in an area of your life, you live in a deficit. If you are clueless about how to live a victorious life in Christ, you live in a deficit. I was in churches that were not preaching holiness or helping to make people accountable. So many leaders get caught up in trying to fill a position in the church rather than making disciples. I know what it feels like to be alone. I can identify loneliness as a single or married woman. The Bible says my people perish for the lack of knowledge. (Hosea 4:6). There are so many of you reading this book, who have found yourself in this same position, many can identify with my pain. After you have had so many disappointments in life, you give up on ever finding true happiness. I honestly believed my life would never get better. I am reminded of what Apostle Paul said; he was encouraging women who were not married to use the time to serve God with their whole hearts because when they are married, their attention is limited. I want to encourage you to put all your trust in God until the right person comes. Work for him, build your intimacy with him, I know it's not easy, and you will fail miserably sometimes. Get back up and keep pursuing God.

I was busy in ministry but depressed and alone. I have heard a lot of people saying that if a single person stays busy in ministry, it keeps them from yielding temptation easily. That is so far from the truth; the enemy waits until you're alone in the early hours of the morning, to confront you with his lies. I had no friends to console me. I always kept to myself, and this my friend made it more challenging. It's always good to have friends in your life, someone you can talk to or pray along with you. We do not have to go through alone.

I was helping Prophetess Sharon in ministry. She had a lot of engagements to minister at different churches in our local area. One night I went to a church where they had a special service. Service was very refreshing and motivating. After the service, we were about to leave when Prophetess stopped to greet one of her colleagues. A gentleman walked up to me and greeted me; he was just polite. I heard a voice saying this is your husband. I rejected that thought immediately because he was not the type of man for me. Even though I rejected the thought, desperation began to set in.

I was leading and bleeding, clueless as to how to get help. I had asked Apostles and Pastors to pray for me to help me out of the pit. It was a faithful Sunday when he walked in, looking like he was wallowing in sorrow. His socks did not match the suit he had on bright red socks. His hair was unkempt, the way he looked made me appreciate where I was. This was the same gentleman that I had seen from time to time at different functions. He asked to meet with me; I obliged him because I could see he was hurting. As

126

he sat at the desk across from me, I heard the voice again telling me he was my husband. It took me a while because we were different, we were like night and day. I begin to compare myself with him; he was not the man for me. As I began to reflect on my life, I came to this conclusion; I am getting what I deserve. Not that he was a bad person, just not the person for me. Who are you to choose? I asked myself; you know no man is going to want you. Just look at you six kids with five different fathers, you better get what you could get.

I was still suffering from rejection and insecurities; I did not know who I was. There was nothing in my life as a child to show me or help me or shape me into a leader. My experience was the total opposite; I was always the outcast; people looked down on me, talked about me, and scorned me. My family was afraid to approach me because I was like a time bomb; you had to tread lightly when approaching me.

The reason I am so transparent is that I went through so much alone. I was offered positions and titles without guidance or instruction. No one ever asked me or cautioned me for the callous life I was living. I was now a Pastor and still struggling. You see, I thought when God promoted me, all the struggles would stop. Leaders nowadays do not take time to help or equip their leadership team. People are being elevated on gifting and not character. I have never had a spiritual father or mother in my life and spiritual sister or brother. Now you may say what is wrong with her. I had a social problem; I was petrified to be amongst a crowd of people at any gathering. People thought I was stuck up, proud, and arrogant. Amazingly Prophets can prophesy, and preachers can preach, members can shout all over the church, yet most churches are lacking empathy and discernment.

I was so broken; I frequently prayed to die. I contemplated suicide on many occasions. I want you to know, yes you are reading this book, that will not be your plight. The Lord has blessed me with a ministry to be a listening ear to people in despair. I am here with prayer warriors, people waiting to talk to you when you can't seem to find a way out.

This *man* that walked into our church was my best option, who would want to be with a woman that has been married four times. I was useless and damaged; no one ever looked at me or even complimented me. I felt useless and

I felt I was waiting on a marriage that would never come. After all, I understood I needed to be married to do ministry; I needed a proper covering.

I began to give into Howard even though I felt he was not the right one. I remembered the voice that spoke to me. Was that God? Of course not, Satan had used this opportunity to further my sorrows. It is so important to have a relationship with God. I mean a deeply intimate relationship, getting to know His voice. I prayed a lot but had not discovered what living a victorious life would suppose to be.

Three voices speak to a person: the voice of God, your voice, and the voice of the enemy. It takes spending quality time with God for one to identify his voice. I was already confused about so many things; it was easy for the enemy to speak to me. I was at my lowest point in life, feeling all hope was lost.

I entertained Howard and felt marrying him was my faith. We had absolutely nothing in common, that did not matter; it was better than nothing.

I helped Howard decide to marry me; I imitated what he completed. I was okay with my fate. Howard did not have any kids, so he was not too familiar with fatherhood. He was married once before, and that ended in divorce. He was a wounded soldier, bottled up and afraid. I took him to some Pastors, to meet him and give us counsel before the marriage. The pastor's wife was taken back when we came through the door. She was uneasy with my decision but later agreed that I had heard God. The wedding was small, only friends and family. I was like a zombie that entire day, felt like I was sentencing myself to a life of misery. I was getting what I deserved.

Early on in our marriage, I recognized he was in a strange place spiritually. I started to see behavior displayed by him that was questionable. It was exceedingly difficult to communicate with him. I realized we were not compatible. You may say you should have seen that from the onset. I was only tired and would have settled with anyone at this point who had agreed. Do not get me wrong Howard is a nice person, just not for me. I was trying my best to love him and treat him right. I prayed night and day and day and night for God to help me. I tried going on dates, having conversations on how to better our marriage. It was all to no avail; I was talking to a brick wall. Howard never talked much about his childhood; one could tell his pain was more outstanding than he could explain. You can never fix a relationship when there is a communication barrier. He was very defensive and argued with just about everything. As the years passed by, I started to develop headaches because of the stress. We had irreconcilable differences, and I know that.

I was still doing ministry alone. My husband's inexperience and inability were not his enemies, but fear of trying and receiving help.

Lord, help me, what do I do. My pain was more significant than I've ever had. People looked down on me because of the man I married. I still yet rise, I run to the rock. Jesus was all I had. I told God that I would remain married despite my unhappiness and being humiliated quite often. I asked God help because sometimes I could be very disrespectful towards my husband. It did not matter the situation. The Bible cautions us to be submissive and honor our spouses.

One day I took a trip home and miraculously heard about a Prophetess there who has a disability but heard from God. God showed me that he wanted me to get a meeting with this woman of God. I did not have an expectation. I was never the one to look or run after prophecy. I always tried to seek God for myself and wait for confirmation. This woman of God confirmed to me that God had not ordained my marriage. She gave me some more details that almost blew my mind; I knew it was God.

My attitude changed, I felt the chains fell off, and God had remembered me. From the moment I knew I could no longer stay in this marriage. I consulted those in authority and told them what God had said. To my surprise, no one disagreed with my decision.

It has been a year since my husband, and I separate. I am waiting for the next move of God in my life. I walk in victory, being able to share my story to help others.

This experience has matured me. I have grown in leaps and bounds. It took me a long time, but I now know who I am. I know God will give me instructions that will bring healing to us all. If you do not remember anything, remember, your past does not define who God calls you to be. You are still a treasure in an earthen vessel. That man will find you and will love you like Christ loves the church. Be patient, and wait. Do not give focus on when and how, but keep your trust in God.

Prayer points to prepare me for God to renew my strength
Bible Reading: 1 Kings 19:1-7
O Lord I worship you for who you are; ever merciful and ever true
Father, I thank you for the miracle of sleeping and waking up
Father, I magnify you for your amazing grace that has kept me thus far in the journey of life

Lord, I thank you for your good plans for my future and the future of my loved ones

O Lord arise and silence every power attacking your glory in my life

O Lord arise and terminate every counsel of the ungodly regarding my destiny in the name of Jesus

Father, I hide in you, immunize me against every aggression directed towards my life and destiny

Just like Elijah, I cry unto you this day, Father, help me in the battle raging against my life and my calling

Father, you did not abandon Elijah in the time of distress, please hear me this day my Lord and my God

When Elijah became weary and discouraged, you fed him with the meal of renewal of strength, Father please feed me with your manna from heaven

Because the Lord is the strength of my life, I shall fear no man, and I refused to be afraid of anything

Today by the strength of the Holy Spirit I receive new power to pick up again every good fight of faith that I have abandoned

Today by the force of the Holy Spirit, my vision becomes sharper and my zeal re-inspired

Today by the strength of the Holy Spirit, I mount up with the wings of an eagle to the mountain of the Lord far above every power of this world

Today by the mercy of the Lord, I triumph over authority and power of darkness arrayed against me and my calling

Thank you, my Father, for answering my prayers in Jesus mighty name

Chapter 7

What should I do while waiting?

It is every girl's dream to get married, have children, and live happily ever after. I remember having such aspirations, waking up with a smile, anxious for my dreams to become a reality.

Marriage was instituted from the garden of Eden between Adam and Eve. God saw that man did not have a companion; he realized it wasn't good for humanity to be alone. He put Adam into a deep sleep and took the woman from one of Adams's ribs; God called her Eve. The woman is created as a helper unto the man; she is to walk by his side, be his support. God gave humanity specific instructions which were to be fruitful, multiply, replenish, and subdue the earth.

God's union of Adam and Eve illustrates God's ideal for marriage—one man and one woman joined together in a life-long commitment to each other, working together to form healthy, godly families. Humankind has not always followed God's ideal way of marriage.

Many persons rush into marriage without first seeking God on the matter and second getting counseling. The Bible declares in Ephesians 5:25-33

25 Husbands, love your wives, even as Christ also loved the church, and gave himself for it;

26 That he might sanctify and cleanse it with the washing of water by the word,

27 That he might present it to himself a glorious church, not having spot, or wrinkle, or any such thing; but that it should be holy and without blemish.

28 So ought men to love their wives as their bodies. He that loveth his wife loveth himself.

29 For no man ever yet hated his own flesh; but nourisheth and cherisheth it, even as the Lord the church:

30 For we are members of his body, of his flesh, and of his bones.

31 For this, the cause shall a man leave his father and mother and shall be joined unto his wife, and they two shall be one flesh.

32 This is a great mystery: but I speak concerning Christ and the church.

33 Nevertheless, let every one of you in particular so love his wife even as himself; and the wife see that she reveres her husband.

This passage of Scripture describes God's heart for marriages. This is not attainable by man; we need God's divine intervention. It is not easy for two people from two different worlds to become one. You must prepare yourself to be a wife by reading the word of God and practical experiences. There are instructions to help us grow the help meet for our spouses. Proverbs 31 gives a clear directive of what God requires of us. This woman in Proverbs 31:10-31 sounds almost like a fairy tale. It's seemed this woman is doing all the work while her husband sits there. This cannot be right. A virtuous woman is in

The Bible in Proverbs 31 describes a virtuous woman as the one who leads her home with integrity, discipline, and more. All the virtues she is practicing are aimed at making the life of her husband better, teaching her children, and serving God.

Who can find a virtuous woman? For her, the price is far above rubies.

11 The heart of her husband doth safely trust in her so that he shall have no need of spoil.

When you are virtuous, your husband will trust with not only his money but his secrets. You will become his best friend. Most times, we can cause a man to shut down because the minute he's starting to communicate, we start to complain and shout. Here's the big one, we never let it go.

12 She will do him good and not evil all the days of her life.

This woman does not keep her body from her husband because of a disagreement. She obeys the word of God, understanding that her body does not belong to herself alone.

13 She seeketh wool, and flax, and worketh willingly with her hands.

She always makes sure her home is taken care of. She beautifies her home, ensuring it is clean and accommodation for her husband.

14 She is like the merchants' ships; she bringeth her food from afar.

Her husband discovers the treasure God has given to him and honors her. She builds her house in love.

15 She riseth also while it is yet night, and giveth meat to her household, and a portion to her maidens.

When her family is hungry, she feeds them. No matter what time her husband wants to eat, she will get up and prepare for him—refusing to ask questions that will cause disagreements. She will not point out that he needs to cook as well; she is tired of cooking. She will build her house because she is wise.

16 She considereth a field and buyeth it: with the fruit of her hands; she planted a vineyard.

Her husband allows her to Purchase properties on his behalf. He trusts her with his money. She will not go shopping for unnecessary items and leave her home depleted.

17 She girdeth her loins with strength, and strengtheneth her arms.

18 She perceiveth that her merchandise is good: her candle goeth not out by night.

19 She layeth her hands to the spindle, and her hands hold the distaff.

20 She stretcheth out her hand to the poor; yea, she reacheth forth her hands to the needy.

This woman is kind and strong. She doesn't use her power to overthrow her husband or manipulate him.

21 She is not afraid of the snow for her household: for all her household are clothed with scarlet.

22 She maketh herself coverings of tapestry; her clothing is silk and purple.

23 Her husband is known in the gates when he sitteth among the elders of the land.

24 She maketh fine linen, and selleth it; and delivereth girdles unto the merchant.

25 Strength and honor are her clothing, and she shall rejoice in time to come.

26 She openeth her mouth with wisdom, and in her tongue is the law of kindness.

27 She looketh well to the ways of her household, and eateth not the bread of idleness.

28 Her children arise up and call her blessed; her husband also, and he praiseth her.

29 Many daughters have done virtuously, but thou excellest them all.

30 Favor is deceitful, and beauty is vain: but a woman that feareth the Lord, she shall be praised

31 Give her of the fruit of her hands and let her own works praise her in the gates.

This woman is everything a man needs to become the king God called him to be.

Spend quality time with yourself, like going to the movies, having lunch, shopping, going to a beauty salon. Check your character, do I want to marry to legalize my sex life or rather to have God's will for a man. While waiting to prepare for your spouse, the first person you want to please is God. If you have learned submission to God, you will get to submit to your husband. This is not easy, especially if he is a man that is unemployed or you make more than he does; you are more educated than he is. Ladies, we tend to define how a husband should be without comparing it with the word of God. While waiting, here is a list of things you can do; love yourself, be the best you God created. Get to know yourself, who am I? What do I like to do? Can I communicate effectively? Become the proverbs 31 women, and God will give you the Proverbs 31 man.

Premarital Counseling Questionnaire

Below are some questions that can be used in your time or at a Women's Fellowship. We must do a deep soul searching before we say I do.

34. How much money do you think you will need to operate your household?

_____

35. Does your wife or husband plan to work?

_____

36. How much money should your mate have for personal expenses (jewelry, athletics)?

_____

37. How often should a family eat out?

_____

38. What part of your family income should be given to the Lord?

_____

39. Do you plan to buy or rent a dwelling?

_____

40. What is your opinion of buying on credit?

_____

41. Which of you is going to handle the money and payment of bills?

_____

42. How much money should be spent on recreational activities?

_____

43. Have you planned any kind of a budget? Will? An insurance program?

_____

44. If she does work and become pregnant, how will the family adjust to the lower income?

45. Do you bring debt into this marriage? If so, how much?

_____

Prayer

Father Lord, in the name of Jesus, I pray for the person reading this that you would preserve and prepare her for her spouse. Lord, don't let her become tired, weary, and accept any person because of the loneliness. Father help her to become the help she needs to become for her spouse. Lord heal her from past hurts and rejection. While she waits on you, God gives her the ability to submit to you. Thank you, Lord, that she will not accept Ishmael; she will wait for her Isaac in Jesus' name. Amen

Books are written by Sherilyn Fletcher

Flawed to Masterpiece

Voices, make them stop!

I'm saved, now what?

Made in the USA
Columbia, SC
27 June 2024

37716870R00090